Maples in the Mist

唐
詩

何
明
方

譯

*For my three wonderful "maples" - Danfung, Mei-Mei and Chris -
who are learning these poems from me by heart now*
—MH

To our daughters, Grace and Ivy
—JT & MT

The illustrations in this book were done in watercolor paints. The display type was set in Fine Hand.
The text was set in Carolina. Printed and bound by Tien Wah Press.
Production supervision by Bonnie King. Designed by Charlotte Hommey.

Lothrop, Lee & Shepard Books, a division of
William Morrow & Company, Inc., 1350 Avenue of the Americas, New York, New York 10019
Printed in Singapore
First Edition   1 2 3 4 5 6 7 8 9 10
Library of Congress Cataloging in Publication Data
Maples in the mist: children's poems from the Tang Dynasty /
[compiled] by Minfong Ho; illustrated by Jean and Mou-sien Tseng.
p.   cm.
Summary: A collection of short poems written over 1,000 years ago
by such poets of the Tang Dynasty as Li Bai, Yin Luan, and Du Mu.
ISBN 0-688-12044-X
[1. Chinese poetry—T'ang dynasty, 618-907—Translations into
English—Juvenile literature.] I. Ho, Minfong. II. Tseng, Jean,
ill. III. Tseng, Mou-sien, ill.
PL2658.E3M36   1996   895.1'1308—dc20   95-17357   CIP AC

CHILDREN'S POEMS FROM THE TANG DYNASTY

Maples in the Mist

張悅珍

曾謀賢

唐 詩

圖

Translated by Minfong Ho
Illustrated by Jean & Mou-sien Tseng

Lothrop, Lee & Shepard Books
New York

唐
詩

自
序

A Note from the Translator

The Tang Dynasty (618-907 AD) is often referred to as the Golden Age of China, when the country was generally at peace and the people prosperous. During this time, the arts flourished and poetry reached new heights of sophistication. In fact, Tang poems are widely accepted as the best classical poems in China's two-thousand-year literary history. There are more than fifty thousand Tang poems known to us, by more than two thousand poets, but by far the best known are the *Three Hundred Tang Poems* selected by a scholar in the eighteenth century. The poems I've translated for this book are taken from this anthology and represent the repertoire of simpler poems traditionally taught to children.

Chinese children have always learned to read by reading poetry. As adults they would be called upon to compose their own poems when they took the civil service examinations or to commemorate important events. Poetry, then, has always been tightly interwoven into the texture of Chinese life.

My own mother made me memorize many of these Tang poems when I was a child—often to her frustration and against my will. I grew up chanting these poems, even before I could read or write, and their simple images have remained vivid in my mind through the years. To me they were tantalizing little windows to a China I had never seen, and they stirred in me a curiosity about and a pride in Chinese culture.

But I never integrated the poems into my everyday life until I tried to teach them to my own children. We were living in rural upstate New York at the time, where our lives seemed nicely interwoven with Tang images—autumn maples and harvest moons, wild geese and snowy mountainsides, solitude and homesickness. In a way, I felt as if I were almost living inside these poems.

My children, however, were more interested in Big Bird on television than in the wild geese of the Tang poems. After forcing my daughter to memorize one short poem, I gave up, feeling as if I had somehow failed my mother. After all, these poems are important to me not only for their beauty, but because they form a part of that strong chain of which I am a link. My mother had recited these poems when she was a child, as had her parents and grandparents before her for more than a thousand years. I did not want to be the weak link in that chain.

And so, in an effort to bridge the linguistic gap between my mother's language and my children's, I began to translate some of the poems from Chinese to English. I don't know of any other English translations done specifically for children. Most were done several decades ago (Arthur Waley's and Amy Lowell's are perhaps the most well known) and as a result sound dated. More recent translations done by the Chinese often sound even more stilted because the translators felt compelled to retain the original rhyme schemes. In contrast, I have opted for a straight, almost literal translation.

In their originals, the poems are short and simple (every Chinese character is monosyllabic anyway, but the choices of words themselves are simple ones) and the syntax is classically symetrical. I've tried to retain the simple vocabulary and, when possible, the parallel syntax, but I've chosen to forego the rhyme schemes and, where they come up, the literary allusions. In most cases, there is no overt subject in Chinese (the "I" is unstated and understood), so, like other translators, I have inserted personal pronouns when appropriate.

In the process of working on this book, my renewed interest in Tang poems has kindled my children's, and they have memorized a few of these poems in Chinese. Is it too much to hope that another generation of children will come to learn and love these poems, and eventually teach them to their own children as well, in one long unbroken chain?

唐詩

自序

On the Pond

Little rascals paddle a little boat
Picking white lilies to steal home.
Don't you know how to hide your trail?
Your boat opens up a path in the duckweed!
—Bai Ju-Yi

唐詩

【池上 白居易】

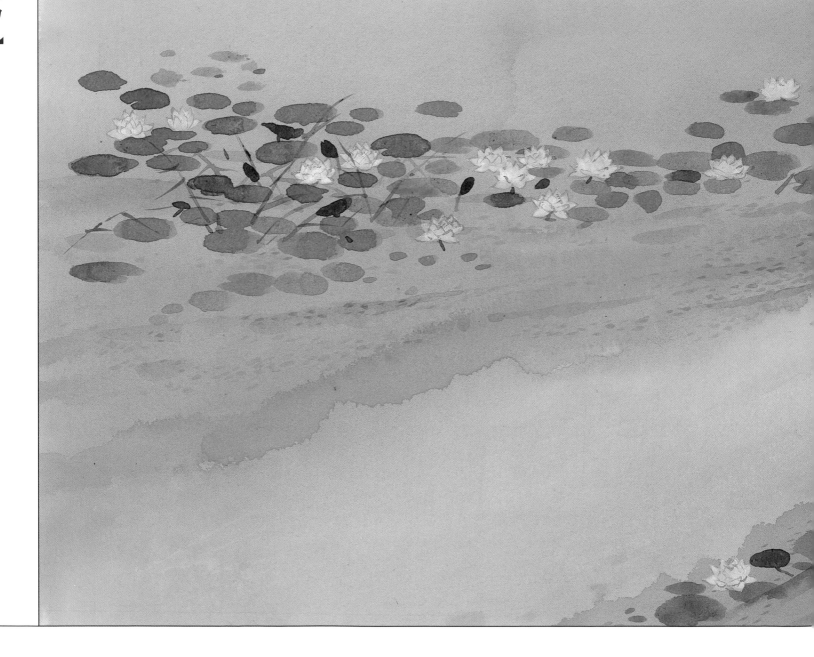

小娃撐小艇　偷採白蓮回　不解藏蹤跡　浮萍一道開

唐詩

【 小松 王建 】

小松初數尺

未有直生枝

閒即傍邊立

看多長卻遲

Little Pine

My little pine tree is just a few feet tall.
It doesn't even have a trunk yet.
I keep measuring myself against it
But the more I watch it, the slower it grows.
—Wang Jian

唐詩

【古朗月行　李白】

小時不識月

呼作白玉盤

又疑瑤臺鏡

飛在碧雲端

Moon

When I was little
I thought the moon was a white jade plate,
Or maybe a mirror in Heaven
Flying through the blue clouds.

—Li Bai

唐詩

【楓橋 張繼】

Maple Bridge

The moon drops, a crow cries, frost fills the air.
By a fishing lamp beneath the river maples I try to sleep.
Then from Cold Hill Temple outside of Ku Su Town
The sound of the midnight bell reaches my drifting boat.

—Zhang Ji

唐詩

月落烏啼霜滿天　江楓漁火對愁眠　姑蘇城外寒山寺　夜半鐘聲到客船

唐詩

【詠鵝 駱賓王 】

鵝鵝鵝

曲頸向天歌

白毛浮綠水

紅掌撥清波

Goose

Goose! Goose! Goose!
Turn your neck and sing at the sky,
Glide your white feathers over the green water,
Paddle your red feet in the clear waves.

—Luo Bin-Wang

Meeting an Old Man

I met an old man on the road
Whose hair was as white as snow.
We walked a mile or two;
He rested four times or five.

—Yin Luan

唐 詩

【 逢老人　隱巒 】

路逢一老人

兩鬢白如雪

一里二里行

四回五回歇

【 遊子吟　孟郊 】

慈母手中線　遊子身上衣　臨行密密縫　意恐遲遲歸　誰言寸草心　報得三春暉

Traveler's Song

My loving mother, thread in hand,
Mended the coat 1 have on now,
Stitch by stitch, just before 1 left home,
Thinking that 1 might be gone a long time.
How can a blade of young grass
Ever repay the warmth of the spring sun?

—Meng Jia

唐詩

【 尋隱者　賈島 】

唐詩

松下問童子　言師採藥去　只在此山中　雲深不知處

Looking for a Hermit

When asked, the little boy under the pine
Says simply, "My master's gone to gather herbs
Somewhere high up in these mountains,
But the clouds are so thick, I don't know where."

—Jia Dao

唐 詩

【春曉 孟浩然】

春眠不覺曉 處處聞啼鳥 夜來風雨聲 花落知多少

Spring Sleep

Sleepily waking to a spring dawn
I hear birds singing everywhere.
After last night's wind and rain
How many blossoms have fallen?

—Meng Hao-Ran

Riverside Song

Alone by the river the wild grass grows.
High up in the deep woods the yellow orioles sing.
The spring stream churns with the twilight storm.
Deserted, a single ferry tosses near the crossing.

— Wei Ying-Wu

唐詩

【滁州西澗　韋應物】

獨憐幽草澗邊生　上有黃鸝深樹鳴　春潮帶雨晚來急　野渡無人舟自橫

Symmetry

A pair of golden orioles sings in the green willows,
A line of white egrets flies across the blue sky.
Through my west window, snows of a thousand autumns cap the mountains,
Beyond my east door, boats from ten thousand miles away dot the river.

—Du Fu

唐詩

兩個黃鸝鳴翠柳

一行白鷺上青天

窗含西嶺千秋雪

門泊東吳萬里船

唐詩 【 山行 杜牧 】

Mountain Road

Far up the cold mountains is a steep stone path.
Nestled in the white clouds is a little house.
We stop our cart to sit among the twilight maples;
After the frost, their leaves glow redder than spring blossoms.

—Du Mu

唐詩

遠上寒山石徑斜　白雲深處有人家　停車坐愛楓林晚　霜葉紅於二月花

唐詩

【靜夜思 李白】

床前明月光

疑是地上霜

舉頭望明月

低頭思故鄉

Quiet Night

A moonbeam by my bed
Or frost on the ground?
I look up at the full moon,
I look down and think of home.

—Li Bai

News of Home

You've just come from my old hometown.
You must have some news of home.
The day you left, was the plum tree
By my window in bloom yet?

— Wang Wei

唐 詩

【 鄉事 王維 】

君自故鄉來　應知故鄉事　來日綺窗前　寒梅着花未

清明時節雨紛紛　路上行人欲斷魂　借問酒家何處有　牧童遙指杏花村

Ching Ming Day

It's raining lightly on Ching Ming Day.
On the road the travelers feel forlorn.
We ask if there's a tavern nearby.
The little cowherd points to Almond Blossom Town.

—Du Mu

唐詩

【登鸛雀樓　王之渙】

Climbing Stork Tower

The white sun sinks behind the hills,
The Yellow River rushes to the sea.
Want to see a thousand miles further?
Let's climb a little higher!

—Wang Zhi-Huan

唐詩

白日依山盡　黃河入海流　欲窮千里目　更上一層樓

About the Poets

Bai Ju-Yi (772-846) *On the Pond*

One of China's most popular poets, Bai Ju-Yi was famous in his own lifetime. His almost three thousand poems were copied on the walls of inns and monasteries and sung by the dancing girls everywhere in China. His fame even reached Korea and Japan, where to this day he is honored at a festival every summer.

Born into an educated family in Hunan province, Bai Ju-Yi was recognized as a child prodigy. After passing the imperial examinations at twenty-nine, he served in a series of posts, some of them in far-flung parts of China because his criticism of official policies had offended people in the court.

Bai Ju-Yi's life spanned the reigns of eight Tang emperors, at a time when China was caught in great political instability. He was keenly observant of and sympathetic to the suffering of the people and in later life developed a deep interest in Buddhism.

Du Fu (712-770) *Symmetry*

Du Fu's position as one of China's master poets has gone unchallenged for almost ten centuries, yet he often thought of his own life as a series of frustrations and failures. Born into a family of literary distinction, he grew up with a strong sense of Confucian duty to his emperor and country. Despite this background, however, Du Fu failed the imperial examinations three times. He was finally given a minor position in the Crown Prince's palace when he was forty-three.

At forty-seven, he left the imperial service and settled in Chengdu, where he spent his most peaceful and productive years. Half of his still existing 1,450 poems were written during this period.

During the last five years of his life, Du Fu took a long river journey down the Yangtze. The river might have taken him home to Hunan, but midway he became ill and spent two years at Kwei-Chou, a famous site overlooking two gorges. There he wrote some of his most mature poems. Continuing his journey onto Tung-Ting Lake, he wrote his last poem while lying sick on a riverboat and died shortly after.

Du Mu (803-852) *Mountain Road, Ching Ming Day*

The eldest of a literary family in Shensi, Du Mu was a distinguished essayist and poet. He passed the imperial examinations when he was twenty-five and was duly posted to official appointments in various provinces. There, in famous old cities such as Lo-Yang and Yang-Chou, Du Mu cultivated a reputation for appreciating striking scenery and beautiful women, both of which he wrote about with great delicacy.

Ching Ming Day is an annual spring festival during which families gather to sweep and clean their ancestors' gravesites.

Jia Dao (779-843) *Looking for a Hermit*

One of the later Tang poets, Jia Dao was from Northern China, near what is now Beijing. Many of his poems allude to the mystical interplay between man and nature and influenced the "Ching Hu" style of poetry during the following Sung Dynasty.

Li Bai (701-762) *Moon, Quiet Night*

Generally considered China's single best poet, Li Bai's poems are praised for their flow and energy (known in Chinese literary criticism as *chi* or breath). He spent his boyhood in Szechwan province, but when he was twenty-four, he left home to explore the world of central and eastern China. He only gained imperial recognition decades later, when he was given a position at the famous Hanlin Academy, but he fell out of favor due to court intrigues three years later and returned to the hills. His restlessness and Taoist nonchalance about fame and wealth have become legendary.

Luo Bin-Wang (640-684?) *Goose*

Talented even as a young boy, Luo Bin-Wang wrote this poem when he was only seven years old. He became a restless adventurer and for years wandered all over China. When he was eventually appointed a petty officer, he got involved in an attempt to assasinate the Empress Wu Zetian. When this failed, he disappeared—some say he was killed, others that he became a monk.

Meng Hao-Ran (689-740) *Spring Sleep*

A native of Hupeh, Meng Hao-Ran was about ten years older than Wang Wei and Li Bai, both of whom admired his poetry. When he failed the civil service examination at forty, he took off on a long journey in the mountains of the central Yangtze region and lived as a recluse. Most of his more than two hundred poems were written during this period.

Meng Jia (751-814) *Traveler's Song*

Although his poetry was celebrated in his lifetime, Meng Jia's long life was a series of failures, poverty, and bitterness. His wife and three sons all died young, and he failed the imperial examinations several times before finally passing in his forties. He was then assigned to a minor post, which he lost because of incompetence. He spent the rest of his life living off friends and patrons. Still, he transcended his personal suffering in his poems.

唐 詩

詩人小傳

Wang Jian (766-830) *Little Pine*

Born into a poor family, Wang Jian was a soldier, courtier, official, and recluse during various phases of his long life. His collection of a hundred "Palace Poems" is particularly well known and is said to be based on actual incidents that happened in the emperor Te-tsung's harem.

Wang Wei (701-761) *News from Home*

Renowned as both a poet and painter, it is often said of Wang Wei that "in his poetry there is painting; in his painting there is poetry." His life was not unlike many of the other Tang poets: considered a prodigy in his teens, he was awarded a government post which later led to various promotions and then banishments to remote outposts of the Chinese empire. Unlike many other Tang poets, however, Wang Wei deliberately chose to withdraw from active society for long periods. Even while holding office in the capital, he led the life of a recluse in a mountain hut, where he spent many quiet years studying Buddhist scriptures. His poems reflect both his love of landscape painting and his devout Buddhism.

Wang Zhi-Huan (688-742) *Climbing Stork Tower*

Little is known about Wang Zhi-Huan, although from his epitaph it is evident that he was considered a great poet during his day. Except for six poems, all his work has been lost to us, but those six are rated as exquisite gems of Tang poetry.

Wei Ying-Wu (737-792) *Riverside Song*

A native of the capital city of Ch'ang-An, Wei Ying-Wu served as an imperial guardsman and later in various provincial posts. Wei's poetry reflects the gentle serenity characteristic of the "Idyllic Nature" school.

Yin Luan (dates unknown) *Meeting an Old Man*

Although his simple poem has delighted generations of Chinese children, very little is known of Yin Luan himself.

Zhang Ji (766-830?) *Maple Bridge*

Not much is known of Zhang Ji. He is thought to have come from a humble family and become a civil servant in 799. The actual Maple Bridge in Suchow has been made so famous by this poem that it has, through the centuries, become a place of pilgrimage for poetry lovers.

61x 2/16

CONTENTS

CHAPTER 1

The Great Soul Trial

arly one chilly November morning in 1949, a seventy-year-old Arizona miner and prospector named James Kidd paused outside the door of the four-dollar-a-week shack he rented. He peered upward at the breaking dawn. A loner who lived quietly, Kidd often stood by himself this way, staring at the sky as if transported into a distant world. Sometimes, after a long shift in the copper mine where he worked, he would scramble onto the tin roof of the mine's pump house to study the stars. At those times, a half-quizzical, half-bemused expression would spread across the old man's weathered face, and his eyes would gleam beneath his battered gray fedora.

That same look must have been on Kidd's face as he put a match to his nickel cigar that November morning. Then, shifting the weight of a borrowed pickax on his shoulder, he shuffled out into the daylight. No one would ever see him again.

No one saw him that last morning, in fact, but Kidd's habits, as observed by his neighbors, tended to be as characteristic as they were spartan. His shabby dress, his frugality, his quirky way of skygazing had marked him as something of a benign eccentric. So had his reclusiveness, a trait that helped explain why, at the outset, his disappearance went almost unnoticed. As Kidd had few friends and no living relatives, it was several weeks before anyone even realized that he was missing. But in a greater scheme of things, his vanishing would not go unremarked. It would, in time, spark the oddest courtroom drama in American legal history.

A police investigation undertaken a month after the old man disappeared failed to turn up any clues or evidence of foul play, and, in time, Kidd was declared legally dead. The matter rested that way for a number of years, for it seemed there was little to distinguish Kidd's case from those of the hundreds of other people who end up missing each year. But James Kidd proved to be a man with a secret, one that was uncovered not by a police detective or a private investigator, but by a conscientious public servant named Geraldine Swift.

Several years after Kidd's disappearance, it fell to Swift, an Arizona estate-tax commissioner, to tidy up the few legal formalities connected with his apparent passing. It seemed a routine case; Swift had handled dozens of similar ones during her long career—or so she must have thought. Apparently, the old man had died intestate and without close kin. The normal procedure would be to liquidate whatever scanty assets he might have left behind and turn the money over to the state treasury as unclaimed property. But somehow the matter of the missing prospector began to hold a curious fascination for her. While leafing through the contents of a safe deposit box Kidd had kept, Swift came across a dog-eared photograph of the elderly miner, staring at the camera from beneath his wrinkled hat with an expression that seemed at once befuddled and wise. Something in that enigmatic expression intrigued her. For reasons so obscure that she herself could not articulate them, she delayed sending the case on through the usual channels. Swift decided she wanted to investigate further.

Before long, it began to appear that her instincts were well grounded. There turned up in her mail, flagged to the Kidd estate, a report from the stock brokerage firm of E. F. Hutton, outlining the liquidation of $18,000 worth of stock that had belonged to Kidd. A notation in the report said that a nearly equal amount had been deposited in a special account that represented the miner's accumulated dividends. This startling revelation was quickly followed by others.

Kidd, it seemed, had been a cautious and prudent investor and had maintained various accounts scattered among several banks and brokerage firms. During the following weeks, these institutions reported to Swift an astonishing catalog of assets. James Kidd—the tatterdemalion prospector who had dwelled in a hovel, dined in hash houses, and read borrowed newspapers—had left behind a fortune of precisely $174,065.69—quite a sizable sum by the standards of the 1960s.

At this point, several of Swift's colleagues began to share her interest in the Kidd matter. Some pressure was brought to bear on her to resolve the case. After all, there was no will. Why deprive the state of what was turning out to be a real windfall? Swift resisted, but by 1964—fifteen years after James Kidd's disappearance and more than five years after Swift first became involved with his legacy—

decisions had to be made. It was time to put paid to the old man's earthly ledger. Accompanied by her assistant and two tax auditors, Swift left her office and made her way to the underground vault of the First National Bank of Phoenix, where Kidd's files languished along with hundreds of other unclaimed accounts. At the time, the bank was undergoing extensive reconstruction, worsening working conditions in the already cramped and cluttered vault. The electricity had been shut off, so the chamber not only was thick with construction dust but also was pitch black. Threading her way by the beam of a flashlight amid the canvas bank sacks and stacked cartons, Swift took down—for the last time, she thought—the box containing Kidd's papers. Rifling through the yellowing files, she felt some sadness, as though she were saying farewell to an endearing, if nettlesome, old friend. By

the light of her flashlight she took up the ragged photograph, studying anew the ambiguous James Kidd smile that had so intrigued her for the past five years. She had grown strangely fond of the mysterious old man, and it seemed somehow unjust that the fortune he had so carefully amassed and frugally tended should simply disappear into the state treasury.

With a sigh, Swift replaced the photograph. She picked up a stack of stock receipts, which were bound with a rubber band. She was about to replace them when something fluttered free from the bundle and wafted to the floor. It was a scrap of lined notebook paper, bearing a blocky scrawl that she recognized as James Kidd's hand-

Photographed before his face was weathered by thirty years of prospecting in Arizona's desert, James Kidd looks fresh and dapper. The eccentric loner touched off a lengthy courtroom search for the human soul. Before disappearing in 1949, Kidd wrote a rough, homemade will (right), requesting that his sizable estate be used to scientifically prove the existence of the soul.

ABOUT, NOT OF 1967

58416

Phoenix arizona Jan 2. 2nd 1946

this is my first and only will and is dated the second day in January 1946. I have no. heirs have not been married in my life, after all my funeral expenses have been paid and $100. one hundred dollars to some preacher of the Gospital to say fare well at my grave sell out in full my property which is all in cash and stocks with the E. F. Hutton Co Phoenix some in safety box, and have this balance money to go in a reserach or some scientific proof of a soul of the human body which leaves at death I think in time their can be a Photograph of soul leaving the human at death,

James Kidd

(dated 2nd
January 1946)

Symbols of the Soul

Swirling down only to reverse and uncoil, the spiral with its endless cycle has intrigued humanity from primitive times until the present. Spirals have been used as symbols in numerous cultures throughout the world, from ancient Egypt and Europe to South America to islands of the South Pacific. They have appeared on pottery, coins, and seals, and in cathedrals, mosaics, rock carvings, earth drawings, and even tattoos. Spirals in slightly altered form, as mazes and labyrinths, have been almost as ubiquitous.

Burial mounds in Ireland and Great Britain reveal spirals chiseled into stones and interior walls, and archaeologists have found evidence of an Egyptian royal tomb, dating from 3400 BC, that was constructed in a spiral-like labyrinthine pattern. Centuries-old turf and stone mazes have been found in England and in Scandinavia, and as far back as the fourth century AD, Christians constructed mazes on church grounds.

While the symbol's significance to early humans remains a mystery, some historians believe the unbroken windings of the helix usually had mystical significance regarding the fate of the soul. The confusing pathways of mazes, for example, may have represented the underworld, mapping a route for the soul to follow: The journey to the center of the maze represented death, and the return path symbolized rebirth. Similarly, the mazes of England and of Scandinavia apparently were once the sites of ritual dances and ceremonies exalting the earth's vernal rebirth. And in the myths of New Zealand's Maori tribe, the spiral was thought to assure the soul's passage into the afterworld.

Experts believe the early Christians may have equated the labyrinth's circuitous route with the arduous road to salvation, an idea not unlike one that existed in ancient Greece. Some scholars interpret the Greek myth in which the Minotaur, a bull-headed monster confined within a labyrinth, is slain by the hero Theseus as a metaphor for triumph over death.

On the Mediterranean island of Malta, spirals decorate the prehistoric temple of Hal Tarxien, a place once dedicated to the worship of an ancient fertility goddess.